BOOK ONE

two at one piano

elementary duets
music by JON GEORGE

commissioned by Frances Clark
edited by Louise Goss

Contents

Cover Design: Candy Woolley

© 1969 Summy-Birchard Music
division of Summy-Birchard Inc.
All Rights Reserved   Printed in U.S.A.

ISBN 0-87487-141-7

Summy-Birchard Inc.
exclusive print rights administered by
Alfred Publishing Co., Inc.

A Little Song

Secondo

A Little Song

Primo

The Circus Is Coming!

Secondo

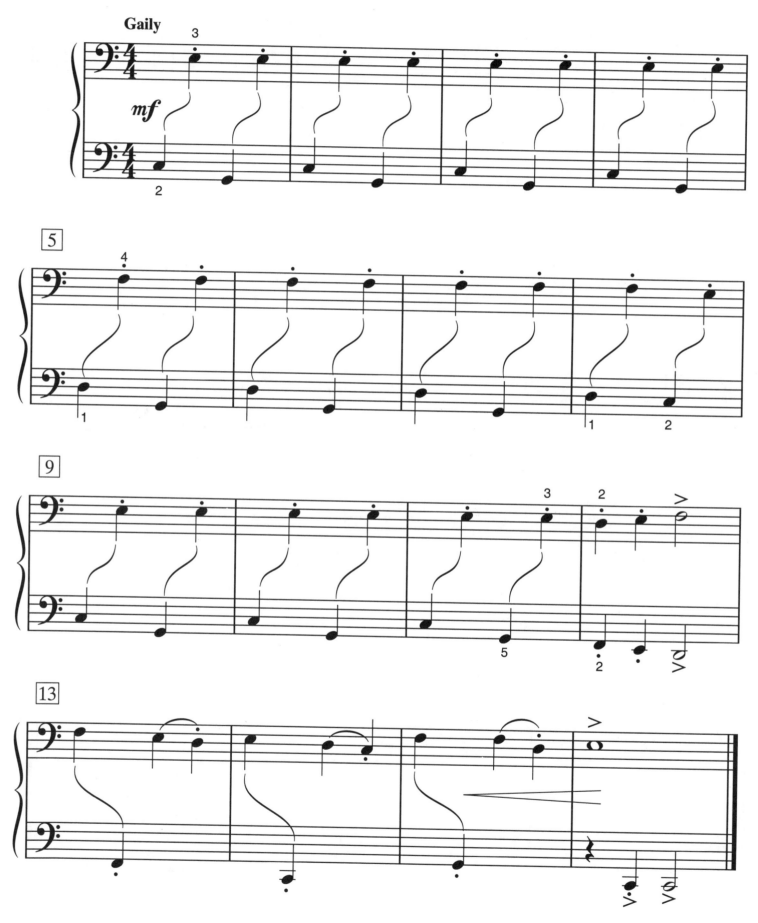

The Circus Is Coming!

Primo

The Sad Butterfly

Secondo

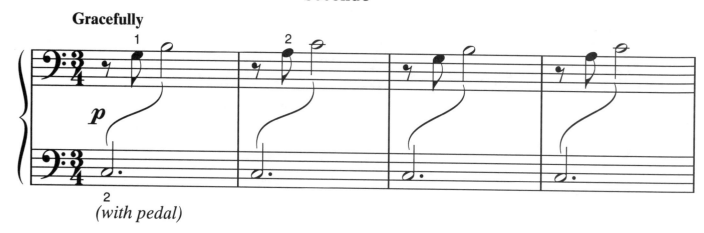

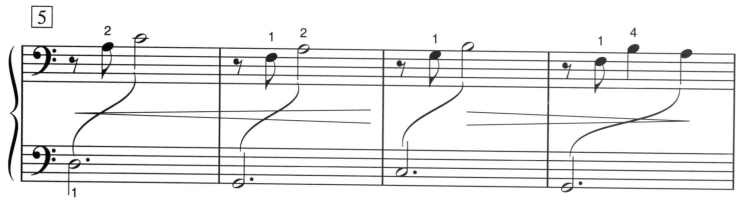

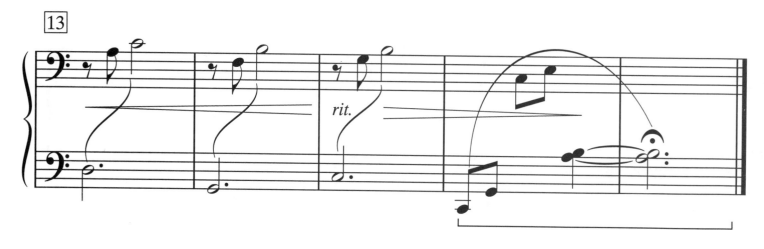

The Sad Butterfly

Primo

Sidewalk Tune

Secondo

Sidewalk Tune

Primo

Crab Dance

Secondo

Crab Dance

Primo

Sunday Afternoon

Secondo

Sunday Afternoon

Primo

Polka Dot Polka

Secondo

Polka Dot Polka

Primo